Contents

CLASSIC FESTIVAL SOLOS, Volume 2 is a counterpart to the companion, Volume 1. Idiomatic solo materials with an eye to variety and playability are included, beginning with easier material and progressing to more difficult.

Works from several periods of composition are presented to give the advancing student the opportunity to learn and to demonstrate performance in each appropriate style. Technical progression is taken into consideration as well as program appeal for both soloist and audience.

Jack Lamb, Editor

DISTRIBUTED BY
ST. ANN MUSIC PUBLICATIONS
St. Louis (314) 427-4453
WATS 1-800-235-9714

TIKI'S TUNE

WALLY BARNETT

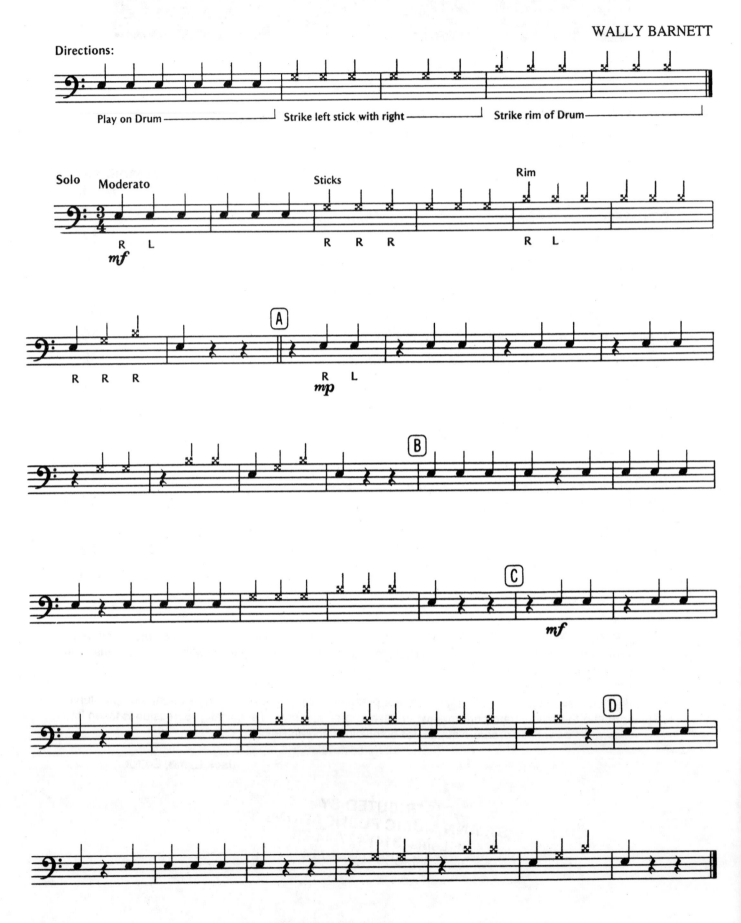

PET ROCK

WALLY BARNETT

FLIM FLAM

WALLY BARNETT

EL03899

SNAP, CRACKLE, POP

WALLY BARNETT

To make a Rim Shot, hold left stick on both rim and drum head and strike with the right stick.

EL03899

DRUMFOUNDED

WALLY BARNETT

Copyright © 1989 BELWIN MILLS PUBLISHING CORP., c/o CPP/BELWIN, INC., Miami, FL 33014
International Copyright Secured   Made in U.S.A.   All Rights Reserved

TRACK SOUTH
(Based on a Mexican Folk Song)

FRED HOEY

Moderate tempo

SWEET ROLLS

WALLY BARNETT

Copyright © 1991 BELWIN MILLS PUBLISHING CORP., c/o CPP/BELWIN, INC., Miami, FL 33014
International Copyright Secured　　　Made in U.S.A.　　　All Rights Reserved

SUGAR BEATS

WALLY BARNETT

EL03899

STICK TO IT

WALLY BARNETT

HIGH SCHOOL CADETS

JOHN PHILIP SOUSA
Arranged by WALLY BARNETT

POLKA DOTS

WALLY BARNETT

GEORGE M. COHAN MEDLEY

GEORGE M. COHAN
Arranged by WALLY BARNETT

*Play all rolls double 16th notes

A HORSE OF A DIFFERENT COLOR

WALLY BARNETT

MARCH 2

KNOHR, SOUSA
Edited by JAMES MOYER
Arranged by WALLY BARNETT

HOEDOWN

WALLY BARNETT

EL03899